Kids' Letters to President Kennedy

Kids' Letters to President Kennedy

Selected by
BILL ADLER

Illustrations by
LOUIS DARLING

William Morrow & Company
New York 1961

Dedicated to all the wonderful American children
represented by the letters in this book

A Note of Thanks

I am grateful to the White House Chief of Mails Thomas R. Padgett and his assistant Marguerite Mondock for their cooperation during my many hours in the White House mailroom selecting the letters for this book.

Bill Adler

Contents

9

Foreword

The letters in this book were selected from many thousands that President Kennedy receives at the White House each week. They were written to him by pre-teen-age youngsters from all fifty states.

It was with a real sense of pride that I undertook this selection, because I believe that these letters are a dramatic example of democracy in action. Where else but in a democracy like ours could a seven-year-old farm girl or a ten-year-old "junior scientist" write to the highest office in the land to speak their minds frankly and without hesitation.

The letters are presented here the way the children wrote them, with their own punctuation, spelling and grammar. To protect the privacy of the writers I have changed their names, omitted their addresses and disguised identifying details such as telephone numbers.

Many of the letters in this book are delightfully humorous—what an antidote they are for the burdensome news we read almost daily in our newspapers. Many other letters are more serious—what renewed faith they give in the young generation of Americans who will some day lead our country.

Children from Maine and Hawaii and all the states in between write to the President on an amazing variety of subjects. These range from exciting bits of news about a pet hamster, dog or cat to surprisingly adult observations concerning the current political scene. Some of the young correspondents make unusual requests of their President; some ask for his advice about the problems of growing up. Some even give him *their* advice on how to handle *his* world problems.

I believe that these letters (which are typical of the thousands the President receives) express a sense of duty, a feeling of patriotism and an interest in our government which should make us proud of America today and very, very heartened about the America of tomorrow.

Bill Adler

Kids' Letters to President Kennedy

1

Getting Personal With the President

American children are far from shy or inhibited when it comes to writing to President Kennedy.

The youngsters tell the President all sorts of personal details about their family life—from news of an Aunt who is about to have a baby in Washington, D.C., to the announcement that a nine-month-old brother has just acquired his third tooth, from confidential information concerning a family argument to their personal feelings about Mrs. Kennedy and Caroline.

What they are doing, what they are thinking, what they are planning—all the news is relayed to the President in uninhibited, candid and delightfully amusing reports on the state of mind of our children today.

Dear Mr. President,

I do not know if you got my last letter. I said in it that I want to be the first man to go to the moon in twelve more years. I know you may not be President then but if your brother Bob Kennedy is give this letter to him.

Thank you
Stanley R————

Mr. Kennedy

I believe God is on the USA side.

Rita S———

Dear Mr. President
   I like you.
   I like your Carolyn and I like your wife. Please
write to me. I love you well by.

                        Love,
                        Sandy F——
I am 7 years old

Dear Mr. President,

I think Mrs. Kennedy is very pretty and very nice. She must be lots of fun.

Your truly,
Nancy R———

Dear Mr. Kennedy,

Do you like the White House? I am seven years old. I like school very much. My mother and dad bought me a new bike. Do you want to see it?

Love
Mitchell T———

Dear Mr. President

My ambition is to be an FBI man. Maybe I will be picked to guard the President some day. I am only 11 years old so it is going to be quite a while.

Sincerely
Arthur A———

Dear President, Kennedy,

I saw your inauguration and I am very happy that you are in office. I hope you have a nice time in office.

And say hello to Mrs. Kennedy for me.

Sincerely
Lawrence J———

Dear Jack,

I have a little brother who is three years old and one who is 9 months old. I was wondering how old your baby was when he started to crawl also I was wondering how old he was when he got his first tooth. My brother who is 9 months old has 3 teeth but doesn't know how to crawl.

Your friend,
Jimmy T———

Dear Mr. Kennedy,
    I am 12 years old. If you need a baby sitter call me (LE 5-3773).

                              Truly yours
                              Annie H———

Dear Pres Kennedy,

My mother and father voted for you. They think you are a very smart man and I think so too. My baby brother is named Billy he is 3. My other brother is named Arthur he is 9. My sister Betsy is 8 and I am 10. My mother and fathers age I don't know.

John G———

Dear Mr. President

You and Jackie are perfect together.

Mary B———

Dear Mr. Kennedy,

I heard that you were a good reader. I am too. I am the faster reader in my class. I can read 725 words a minute and I can understand what it means.

Sincerely yours,
Francis P———

Mr. Kennedy

I am building a rocket. I am 7 years old.

Tommy G——

Dear Mr. Kennedy,

I am glad you are president because all of my school voted for you.

My daddy, Mr. Lester S——— is watching the football game.

My mother, Mrs. Martha S——— is making pickles.

I Joanne S———, is of course I am writing to you.

P.S. Please write back.

Dear President Kennedy,

My name is Carole M———. I think that you are about the best President we ever had. I also like your speeches. The talk you gave about Berlin was very good. I am eleven years old. I am a Catholic. I think your daughter Caroline is adorable and your wife is charming. I do not know much about your baby John.

Sincerely
Carole M———

Dear Mr. President

My name is Jane H————. I am 11 years old and going to the 6th grade. I got this milk cap on a bottle and thought you might like to have it.

                    Sincerely
                    Jane H————

Dear Mr. President,

I read your wonderful book Profiles in Courage. I think it is a most interesting book. I am nine years old and I didn't understand a few words.

                    Sandra M————

Dear President Kennedy,

Our club is called the Happy Days Club. Our club has voted a model member which is you. Please send us your autograph and picture.

Our members have tried to keep our club a secret but it didn't work out that way.

Sincerely yours
Happy Days Club
Madeline, Maureen,
Barbara, Patricia,
Donna, Rita, Lois

Dear President Kennedy,

For a very long time I have been saving my spending money and just a little while ago I was able to buy a share of General Motors stock.

I planned to save more and add it and, when I get older work so that I can go to college and not have to ask help from Uncle Sam or anyone else. I am eleven year old now.

Is my share of General Motors which I have saved so hard to buy soon going to be worth nothing or maybe very little because so much of it has to be sold.

I pray for you. I hope you will help me and all the other people who work hard and save their money.

Lionel H———

. . . I was able to buy a share of General Motors stock.

Dear President Kennedy,

Saturday evening July 12th as I was viewing the Washington Monument, three helicopters flew over and landed on the White House lawn then took off. Were you in either of them, if so which one?

I enjoyed visiting Washington very much.

Please answer.

A friend,
Lee R————

Dear Mr. Kennedy,

My name is Aileen P————. My father is chief in the Navy. Before you were elected President of the United States families could not travel with their fathers. I would like to thank you for changing that law.

Yours truly,
Aileen P————

P.S. I hope you can read my writing. My age is 9½ years old.

Dear President Kennedy,

I would like to tell you that I think you are doing a wonderful job for our country. You have already made great improvement for our country in the short time you have been President! My family and I would like to tell you that whatever decision you make about Berlin we know it will be the best for all of us. I know you need all the prayers you can get so here is a Spiritual Bouquet offered for you.

Masses, Rosaries, Our Father, Hail Marys

| 5 | 5 | 10 | 10 |

                    Thank you,
                    my gratitude and luck
                    Maria D————

Dear Mr. President

Ever since mom and dad saw you on TV they fight. Mom wants to make a shelter and dad says no because he just went back to work and theres to many bills to pay.

Mom crys all the time. They fight almost every day. If I were biger I would buy them this one for their anniversary in February. Then they will be happy.

Joseph O———

Dear Mr. Kennedy

Hi! You don't know me, my name is Ann P———. I'm nine. I go to school in Denver.

My family is something like yours, except we have six kids in my family.

Good by,
Ann

P.S. I'm Catholic, too

Dear Mr. Kennedy

My friends and I would like to know if we could have a real FBI Club. We have started a childrens FBI Club. If we can just send me a letter addressed from yourself.

Yours truly,
James P———

P.S. Please don't mind my writing

Dear Mr. President,

Do you wear a hat and like the White House and Washington? I want to buy my Daddy a hat like yours for his birthday. I love you a lot and your family. I think you are very handsome and so is my dad.

Betty S———

Age 9

Dear Mr. Kennedy

I am sending a picture of A. Lincoln since you and Lincoln are both Presidents in the 60's.
Lincoln—1861
Kennedy—1961

Andrew N———

Dear Mr. Kennedy,

You are cordially invited to a mass football rally and bonfire to be held at our High School. The date is October 11. Please bring Jackie and Caroline.

Yours truly,
George R———
President, Student body

Dear Mr. Kennedy,

We are two 11 year old girl admirers of yours. We were rooting for you all the way and were overjoyed when you won the election.

My name is Rowenna and my girl friends name is Shirley. We live across the street from each other and about 20 min from Cincinnati.

We are quite populor with the boys and we don't mind that one bit.

We enjoy bowling, chess, sketching and babysitting.

We just wanted to tell you how very much we like you. Please write to us.

Yours very truly
Rowenna and Shirley

P.S. Since there are two of us could you please sign your name twice? Thank you.

Dear Pres Kennedy,

We have started a club in your favor. We have named it the Kennedy Friendship Club. We have wrote a song called Kennedy Friendship Song. We hope you like it. We live in Philadelphia. Our President (not you) of our club is Joan D———. Our vice president is a four year old she is my little sister her name is Diane. Secretary is me. Treasurer is Marlene J———. Better be going.

Goodbye
Love
Elaine D———

P.S. We would love to sing it for you someday soon.

43

Dear Mr. Kennedy,

How is everything in Washington D.C. I was just reading the newspapers and your last speech was wonderful.

The main reason I'm writing to you is because I think you need cheering up. That is why I will tell you about my vacation.

I am having lots of fun water skiing and swimming in the lake. The fishing is wonderful. I wish you were here too.

Your loyal friend,
Harry S———

Dear President and Jacqueline Kennedy,

I would like to introduce myself. My name is Jill T———. I am 9 years old. Please send me a picture of both of you and the children.

Today while my aunt was driving her car a lady skid and bumped the door. Its all smashed and the window is cracked. (lucky she has saftey plate glass) She wasn't hurt at all. I can't think of anything else to write.

Love
Jill

2

Questions Even the President May Find Difficult to Answer

One statement you can make about the youngsters in this country without fear of repudiation is that they ask more questions about more different things than any nation of children under the sun.

And they seem to direct the most off-beat questions to the President of the United States.

The trivial and the important—the serious and the comic—all questions seem to land right on the President's desk. Some of the questions the youngsters have written to the President are personal—about his family and his life. Others deal with the business of running the country.

It would take more men than currently staff the Pentagon to answer these youngsters' queries.

Surely President Kennedy would need his wisest advisors to find an appropriate reply for the nine year old boy who asked—in all sincerity—"What are Presidents for?"

As you read these letters you may begin to wonder where in the world they get all the questions—they are so unusual. I'm afraid that's one question to which only the children know the answer!

Mr. President,

I noticed you have written several stories and had them published. I am very interested in writing. I hope to someday become a writer. How do you get the public to notice your writing?

Sincerely
Carole B———

Dear Mr. President,

Would you please tell me what your confirmation name is?

> Thank you
> Harvey J———

Dear Mr. Kennedy,

I am 8 years old and I'm much interested in your family in the White House.

Could you tell me how it is to be President of the states? and having a car that the seats raise up and a plane that is private.

> Love,
> Carol G———

Dear John,

Could you tell me how to make money so I can get a go-kart.

Harold P———
Age 8

Dear President Kennedy,

I am writing to ask you a question which no one I know can answer. Here is the question,

Why are we trying to get to the moon?

I would appreciate an answer if you have the time.

Thank you.

Sincerely

Charles K———

Dear Pres Kennedy,

Do you ever get breakfast in bed?

Yours truly
Larry D——

Dear Mr. Kennedy,

I am 9 years old. I want to know if you are for or against Communism.

Carol F———

Dear President Kennedy

I would like to know of your hobbies and spare time activities if you have any.

Respectfully yours,
Ted N———

Dear Mr. Kennedy,

I am very glad I can write to you. What have you been doing this summer?

My friend, Stanley K——— wants to know what you've been doing this summer too.

Say hello from me to Mrs. Kennedy too.

Sincerely,
Richard D———

Dear Mr. President

I have a picture of you and your hair is parted on the right side. We went to the *Wax Museum* and it was parted on the left side. Which side is right?
Thanking you in advance I remain

Very truly yours
Ann L———

Dear Sir

How does it feel to be President? Have you told your daughter that she does not live normally? (that most people do not live like she does?)
Is your wife ever going to change her hair do?
I am a ten year old boy. Thank you very much.

Sincerely
Alex N———

Dear President Kennedy,

This is Hannah M———. I am nine years old and in the fifth grade. I would like to know why we don't have girl military school. Because I want to go to one.

Your friend,
Hannah

Dear Mr. Kennedy,

I have been wanting to write but I have never got to it. I wanted to ask if a 11 year old boy could get a job washing dishes at a cafe to earn some money? The reason I asked you because I need some money to pay for tire for my bike. I am glad you were elected cause if Nixon was elected we would have a lot sooner war. Cause when Cruchef beat the table with his shoe Nixon just laught. And when you put your return address put it in your own hand writing. I will send a picture of me to show what I look like.

A good friend
Yours truly
Bill C———

Dear President Kennedy,

I am a boy that you might call a wonder of the future. And I would like to ask you some questions.

1) Do you wish to be president in the 64's and 68's?

2) Do you like being president? Does your wife?

3) Do you like living in the White House? Is it fun?

4) What does Vice President do when your their to take over?

I guess that's all for know.

Yours truly,
Harvey E———

P.S. My writing is not so good, is it?

Dear President,

Will the law permitt me to go deer hunting and hunting at my age of 9?

Would you please answer me. I would like the deer heads in my room. Thank you.

Sincerely

James D———

Dear Mr. President

I am an 8 year old boy. I was wondering if you had the time to answer my question.

Could you please tell me what taxes are for.

From
Jeffry H———

Dear Mr. Kennedy,

How are you? What are you doing in Washington?

Your pal,
Harry S———

Dear Mr. Kennedy.

Please answer this question for me. What are Presidents for? Thank you.

                              Yours truly,
                              Richard S———

3

Dear President Kennedy,
I Want to Shake Your Hand

The youngsters who have written to the President are flexible. Although many of them want to meet the President in person, they offer Mr. Kennedy a choice: either they will come to the White House to meet him or he can come to their house to meet them.

Less fearless mortals (adults) would probably not approach the President with a request for a personal meeting with the same directness these youngsters have employed in their letters to President Kennedy.

Then again, we adults might not dare to request a meeting with the President at all. That is something which is reserved for the leaders of Congress, the Secretary of State or Defense or a bright eyed seven-year-old girl from Wyoming who won't take "no" for an answer.

Dear Mr. President

I have a paper called the Local Town News. I would like some important news. May I come to one of your press conferences for news. My mother and father both voted for you and think you are a good president.

Sincerely yours
Thomas N————

P.S. I have sent you one of my papers

Dear President Kennedy,

I am nine years old. The only Presidents in my life are you and Mr. Eisenhower. I was wondering why you never visited my neighborhood.

My brother who is 7 years old would like to shake your hand.

Lois T————

Dear Mr. President

I would like to make reservations about coming to see you and meet you in the White House. What days do you get off from work so I can see you.

Truly,
Francis S———

Dear President Kennedy,

I know how busy you are, but if you could get me to the White House I'll explain my plan for the Cubans.

Your friend
Micky M———

Dear Mr. Kennedy,

One of my greatest ambitions, next to going to heaven, is to shake hands with you.

Sincerely,
Harold D————

Dear Mr. President,

Would you come to Dallas and come to my house and bring the kids.
The kids can go swimming at the pool.

Herbert T———

Dear Mr. Kennedy,

I would like to ask you if one is allowed to visit the White House and if not why? Age 10.

Yours truly
Victor A———

Dear Mr. President,

I recieved the picture that you sent me and like it very much. Someday I may be able to come to the White House.

The closest I have ever gotten to it was on July 28th (my birthday) when I went over to the gates. There I saw Carolines ducks. I bet she has a lot of fun with them. But my favorite things are cars and trucks. By the way, we will be moving to Chicago in a few weeks. When we move I will write to you and tell you what it is like. Well, it is dark and after my bedtime so I think I'll say goodbye.

Sincerely,
Julio S———

Dear Mr. President

The best thing I would like to do is to have a conference with you. I know you can not because you are so busy working for our government but would you please write to me and send me an autographed picture.
How is your family?

Your friend
Jimmy D————

Dear Jack,

I sure do want to see you a lot. You see I've never seen a president in person and I want to you.

Conrad G————

4

The President Receives Advice

Nowadays the President of the United States can expect advice from everywhere and everybody. But nothing can compare to the advice that President Kennedy has been receiving in his mail from children all over the country.

The youngsters' suggestions range from advice on how the President can improve the condition of his bad back to youthful thoughts on the value of trying to reach the moon.

After reading these letters of advice to the President you may wonder if you have been missing a good bet all these years—and even think that perhaps the next time you need some advice you should really turn to your children.

If these letters to President Kennedy are any indication, the advice you receive may amaze and delight you.

Dear President Kennedy

Instead of trying to reach the moon, why don't scientists try to find out what causes the viruses and other diseases.

Sincerely yours
Fred F———

Dear Mr. President,

I am writing in regard to ex president Eisenhower. The news men and people say President Eisenhower. I think he should be presented as ex President Eisenhower or Mr. Eisenhower.

In saying "President Eisenhower" this way takes away from your title as the one President of the United States.

I hope there is some way of adjusting this if it be a mistake.

Yours truly
Herbert B———

Dear Mr. Kennedy,

I think we should have missiles in boxcars so if a Russian plane is coming over the United States it gets blown up or we should talk to Mr. Khrushev and tell him we will surrender if he lets us live like we want.

Yours truly,
Victor M———

Dear Mr. President,

I wonder why stores are closed on Sunday and not on Saturday. God rested on the seventh day not on the first, so Saturday is the Sabbath.

I love America and have lived in it all my life. I think it is wonderful, but the U.S. is meaner than it thinks. I agree that a person who does wrong should be punished, but the Electric Chair is too much.

Natalie R———

Dear President,

If you try to tax savings dividends whats going to happen to children. I don't have much right trying to tell you something like this.

But what about my future. If taxes go up higher I might not be able to go to college.

Bea M———

Dear Mr. President,

I think you were doing the right thing when you signed the bill for future space ships.

I am pretty sure you know my Uncle Jack or John J———. He was campaning for you in town.

Yours truly
Holly M———

Dear Mr. Kennedy

You may think this is silly but I was wondering
if you would listen to something I have to say.

Would you let me be on planes that might be
hijacked and let me try to help out if someone tried
hijacking a plane.

Sincerely yours,
Ira P———

Dear Mr. President,

I know you already asked Secretary Arthur Goldberg to stop the fight about the Metropoliton Opera Co. but that didn't do very good. Could you please ask Dean Rusk and Vice President Johnson. If that doesn't work look into it yourself.

P.S. I'm 12 years old.

Bunny D———

Dear Mr. Kennedy,

I have been thinking real hard and I think that a woman president would be very nice in the White House.

But she should be young about 40 years old, smart like a teacher, very pretty indeed and intelligent.

There is just one more thing. I think that school should be three months and vacation nine months. Don't you think so?

Then you could see your children more often.

Yours truly
Edna N———

Mr. Kennedy,

I feel that the money that you are spending is within good reason. I also feel that with you and Mr. Johnson in office our taxes are going to better use.

Sincerely,
Howard C———

My dear Mr. President

I am a 11 year old, listening to the 7:30 report on news today September 18, 1961 heard there was to be a \$15–20,000,000 aquarium put into the Capitol building if all agreed on it.

Think what we could do with \$15,000,000 in this day and age.

With war practicaly staring us in our face we should invest our money in something worth while instead of some big fish bowl.

I agree with those who don't want the aquarium. I hope you agree with me.

Sincerely
John N———

Dear Pres Kennedy

How are you. Fine I hope. Getting down to business. I think it is unfair not letting us have firecrackers on the fourth of July.

So I hope this coming 4th of July you should let us have them and if too many kids get hurt you could stop it.

Yours truly but not
a taxpayer yet
I speak for all of us.
  Stephen M——— (me)
  Mitchell M———
  Robert M———
  Alfred D———
  Teddy D———
  Larry D———

Dear Kennedy,

I feel sorry for you having a bad back like yours.
I think you should lie down when your home and
have a lot of sleep.

Your friend
Rudolph F———

Dear Sir,

As it would be proper to have introductions made
at a meeting let me introduce myself. My name is
Nina G———. I have not written you to pester you
with problems or crazy threats. I just want to give
you a word of encouragement.

You are truly a lucky man to have such a family
to change the subject.

Best of all wishes,
your admirer
Nina

Dear President Kennedy

I would like to pass a law that a child can work in the summer, but if the child dose not do good work, the owner of the store can say get out.

I hope you will pass my law.

Your friend,
Perry H———

P.S. If you can't pass the law it is to bad, but I'd like it very much if you would pass the law.

Dear President Kennedy,

Freedom of the Press is good but you are loosing your private life to the press. You can't do anything without the press on your trail.

I would never be president unless my life and my relatives life was closed to the press.

I'm glad your housekeepers won't tell the press what your private time contains.

Yours truly
George R———

Dear Mr. President,

I saw a picture of you on vacation at Hyannis Port. In the picture I see that you are crossing in the middle of the street. In the future I hope you will cross at the cross walk.

Respectfully yours,
Marsha L———

Dear Mr. Kennedy,

I think you are doing a good job even if that rat Castro is making it hard. Well now for business. I think you should do something about the milk strike in Chicago. You probably have all the milk you wanted when you were a boy. So think of other people.

Dean K———

Dear Mr. President

I read in a magazine that you don't open your own mail.

You mean you can't open your own letters addressed to you? After all you are the President. I think you should open your own mail.

Sincerely yours
Larry B———

Dear Mr. President,

How are you? How is your wife and children. I hope they are fine.

In some of the pictures that I see of you you look tired. You know you have to stay healthy for your country and your family.

I guess your summer probably hasn't been too pleasant with this Berlin Crisis.

The people have faith in you Mr. President and whatever is decided concerning it I'm sure it will be in the best interest for everybody.

Sincerely
Arthur D———

Dear President,

    I think we should use a water bomb to wash our enemys out.

Thank you
Jimmy M———

Dear Mr. President,

I know you probably won't be reading this personally but I hope it might be anway. I was wondering if I could have an autographed picture of you and your wife Jacqueline?

When you were a senator my sister wrote you two letters on the religious matter and politics. I was just wondering if you remembered. You might not but then you might because you have such a good head for most everything else. I think you'll make a very good President but you should be more attentive to your wife, that's important too. If you want to make the people happy you should make your wife happy.

But I won't butt in on family affairs 'cause I know what happens if somebody does. I'd be very happy if you'd write something about our progress as citizens, so I could take it to school.

Thank you.
Lawrence D———

5

Some Unusual Requests

If the President were to fill all the requests he receives in his mail from children the federal budget would have to be doubled.

Even the President would have a difficult time explaining to Congress that he needs more money so that he can satisfy all the youngsters who have asked for samples of the napkins used in the White House, or for a new American Flag with fifty stars.

Not all the requests made of the President require dipping into the Federal Treasury. Many of the youngsters have written to President Kennedy to ask for his assistance on a personal problem. Other children want his official intervention on a pressing neighborhood problem. But no matter how—they expect his help.

After all, what is a President for, the young correspondents reason, if he can't help a seven-year-old girl in distress or a nine-year-old boy who needs some help for his Little League team.

Dear President Kennedy,

The boys on my street are so rough and rowdy that something must be done. Larry J——— is their leader of them. He is also mean. I know you have problems about Cuba and Berlin but will you stop them.

                              Sincerely
                              Mary O———

Dear Mr. President

    I have 50 Pen pals. If you write to me I will have 51.

                    I hope so
                    Joan T———

Dear Mr. Kennedy

    At camp we talked about a problem of beer bottles being tossed out on peoples farms and land. In the city they get tossed out in the streets. I would like to know if you could do anything about this problem. Please write back soon.

                    Yours truly
                    Russ K———

Dear Mr. President

I know this won't seem very important to you but it really means a lot to me. I would like a week dedicated to my favorite singer, his name is Jackie Wilson. He sings rock and roll.

We want the week of August 15th but really anytime would be alright.

Yours truly
Hilda M———

Dear President,

I would like to know the address of X vice president Nixon. I know yours by heart.

Thank you,
Philip G———

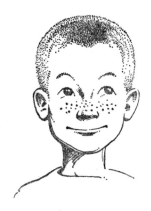

...a haircut like yours.

Dear President Kennedy,

I am a nine year old boy. I have seen you on TV and I like your haircut very much. I often ask my mother if I may have a haircut like yours. I wonder if you could write back and advise my mother to get me a haircut like yours.

Yours very truly,
Wiley M———

Dear Mr. Kennedy

I have just started a stamp collection in the ex-
plorer stamp album and I was wondering since you
get so much mail if you could save some foreign and
odd looking stamps for me.

Thank you
Roger M———

Dear Mr. President,

I would like permission to have a tractor to knock
down 11 trees. The reason we want them knocked
down is for a baseball field across the street from my
house.

If this is permitted we boys will be very grateful.

Thank you
Sincerely
Jay B———

Dear Mr. Kennedy,

May I have a picture of you and your wife.

Thank you,
Dick C———

If it cost anything please send back and tell me.

Dear Kennedy,

Please don't let tax stamps be ruled out. Our school gets beautiful things with money from tax stamps. *Please try!* Please answer this letter. Good Luck.

Kathryn N———

Dear Sir

Would you get Channel 4 to put The Lone
Ranger on TV. Here are the people that want them.

    Patty L———
    Jeffrey L———
    Michael L———
    Francine D———
    Patricia D———
    Alison D———
    Linda Sue D———

                    Yours truly
                    Nancy D———

Dear President Kennedy

My name is Billy B———. I am eight years old. Will you please send me a bycycle. I have never own one. My parent is not able to get me one. Please Kennedy. Send me a bike. One day I am going to be a president just like you. I will help all the boys and girls that write to me. This is all from Billy. Goodby.

Dear Mr. President

I am a boy 10 years old and would like to go to military school but don't know how to get in the school. Will you please help me. I don't have any money to pay. My mother she is a widow.

I would also like to be a Catholic.

Yours truly
Martin M———

Dear President Kennedy,

I'm a 11 year old farm girl. I collect napkins and I have 125. I would like very much to have one of your napkins.

My address is

Maureen H———

Dear Mr. Kennedy,

My name is Larry D———. I am from Troop 239 of New York. I am writing about the boy scouts. I have to have a sponser because you have a sponser for the Eagle Banquet. So I wanted to know if you would be my sponser. The scout office always picks the sponsers but they said you could be my sponser if you want to.

A life Scout
Larry D———

Dear President:

Could you send me a new flag. I had one but somebody stold it.

My address is Alan D————, Chicago. Are we going to have a war. Please send me a flag.

Thank you,
Alan D————

Dear Pres Kennedy

I have a collection of business cards and I was wondering if you have a business card for my collection.

One of your citizens
Tobey E————

Dear President Kennedy,

I would appreciate all of the information you can get on being an astronaut.

Sincerely yours,
Howard B———

Dear Mr. President,

I have missed most of your speeches because I was studying my Boy Scout Handbook.

I would like a copy of your speeches especially about the Berlin crisis.

Eugene E———

Dear President Kennedy,

I want the names of the people that are Communists in the United States.

Your friend,
Frank S———

Dear Sir,
I am studying about the Western Hemsiphere in school so could you send me as much information as possible on it to me.
Thank you.

Douglass F———

Dear Mr. President,

My name is John N————. I am 12 years old. I was wondering if you might see your way clear to send me a bicycle.

You see my Mother works, my Fathers disabled and can't my sister and I have diabetes, and my two aunts live with us. Don't get me wrong, we are not poor or anything but do have a lot of bills to meet. I realize that you are a busy man and probably could not do this but if you could I'd really appreciate it. I could also use a set of electric trains. Either one. I am very sorry to ask you to do this but your my only and last hope.

Well I don't think you the kind of man to ignore my plea.

Your everlasting little friend,
John N————

Dear Mr. Kennedy

Will you please send me a picture of the men that went into space and the rockets. And the three men that are going to the moon and that rocket.

Margaret F———

Mr. President,

I wonder if its possible if you could ask your brother in law Peter Lawford for a picture of him and his autograph.

Best wishes,
Ruth T———

6

The Very Young Politicians

Obviously the statement that "Politics is everybody's business" is taken literally by our young citizens.

They were active participants in the recent Presidential campaign and some vigourous views on that campaign are expressed in their letters to the President.

Many youngsters have obviously got their eye on the Presidential election of 1992 and from the tone of these letters we should have a pretty hot and exciting campaign that year.

Dear Mister Kennedy

My name is Danny H———. I am 10 years old and 5 feet 2 inches tall. I am a person who wanted you to become ·president. Before you became president just about all my room wanted Richard Nixson. But Craig N——— and I fixed that and this is how we did it we made up a speech and this is it.

If we were grown ups we would want a President with a good personality. We would want him to be smart and young so we could keep him for a long time. Also a man who play games like football when he was a boy and thats what John F. Kennedy did and then we took a vote and you won by ten votes.

The reason we brought a game like football into the speech is because we think a person who would play games as a boy would be a good president.

Truly a Democrat
Danny H———

. . . we made up a speech and this is it.

Dear Mr. President,

I hope you are feeling well. I am nine years old. In the election I wanted you. I'm glad you are our President. I am going into the second part of the fourth grade.

Today I went downtown to get my hair cut. I was going to go to Washington except my aunt that I was going to visit is going to have a baby.

Sincerely yours
Nicky R————

Dear Jack

I would like to know how you got to be President.

Your friend,
Dick W————

Dear Sir,

How long do you think it will be before there will be a lady President in the White House?

Yours truly,
Rita E———

Dear President Kennedy,
I am 12 years old and going into the seventh grade. At our school, when your in seventh, you learn about the bodies, its members (at the present) its use, and sometimes, its history, that make-up our government.
I was wondering if you (or who ever can) could send me a little report on each body that makes up our government.

Thank you
Yours truly
Alfred F———

Dear Mr. President

Why can't you have page girls as well as page boys for girls that are interested in the government.

Sincerely
Debbie H———

P.S. If they ever have Page girls I want to be one.

Dear Mr. Kennedy

I did not watch when you became Pres. nor did we vote for you and we didn't like you cause you were too young. But today guess you do as much as any other Pres would do. My brother and sister don't like you that much.

I like you so cheerup.

A week from now I am going to school. Well gotta leave now.

Bye and good luck
Joyce O———

Dear Mr. President

    I think you are the second best president we ever had.

Sincerely
Peter G———

Dear Mr. Kennedy

When you came to Honesdale, Pennsylvania to make a campaign speech my brother Skipper threw a rabbits foot in your car. Aren't you glad?

Love

Martin S———

Dear President Kennedy,

I admire you deeply. I think you are handling the world situation nicely. There is one question that has been puzzling me.

"How does a person get into politics?"

I would be very grateful if you or someone in your cabinet would answer my question.

Thank you
Stanley D———

Dear Mr. President,

I told my sister that I wanted to be the president of the United States in the future. When I said this she laughed and said I could not because to become President you have to know all the capitols of the states. Which I do not.

Do you have to know all of them before you can be president? Do you know them?

Yours truly,
Jane M———

Dear President Kennedy

What mistakes did Mr. Nixon make?

Yours truly,
Henry B———

Dear Mr. President

.My name is Frank G————. I am eight years old. In school we had an election. I voted for you. You won in our room. I was very happy. Please write to me soon.

Love,
Frank

The President
The Honorable John Fitzgerald Kennedy
The White House
Washington 25, D. C.

My Dear Mr. President,

My name is Andrea G———— and I am a freshman in high school.

I would like to have some information about the life of a Democratic President and his family. And maybe a picture. I have some information on a Republican President but I am interested in the Democratic party. My parents are Democrats and I wanted you to win all the way.

Respectfully,
Andrea G————

Dear John,

I am a little late but I am sorry that Kentucky went for Mr. Nixon.

Bruce G———

President Kennedy

I am 13 years old and will be in the 9th grade.
I am going into the army and am very interested
in politics. I've no father or mother, brother or
sister. My home is with 3 aunts and my grand-
father.

If I could have my choice of a father it would
be you.

Thankfully a citizen
Stewart M———

Mister President

I admire the work you are doing. I think the people were right to vote for you in the election.

Oh, yes, how does it feel to be the 35th President of United States? Well I have to go now by.

A good admirer
Lyn G———

P.S. See you on TV

7

The Animal Kingdom

President Kennedy probably knows more about dogs, pigeons, snakes, cats, cows, ponies, rabbits, mice and monkeys than any man in the country—thanks to the remarkably descriptive letters on the animal kingdom which the President receives from his young correspondents.

Obviously if the voting age were lowered to eight, any President running for re-election would have to know as much about raising hamsters as he does about balancing the federal budget or he'd lose the vote of about 98% of the country's children.

Naturally, pets mean problems for some youngsters and they expect their President to have a ready solution.

When a seven-year-old girl writes to the President about her cat who is about to be a mother for the eleventh time and asks for his personal advice—this is the highest tribute any man can receive.

Dear President Kennedy,

I had a girl cat named Princess and my Mother said we had to give it away because it had four kittens before and six in April. My Mother put Princess and one of her kittens losse in the country without letting me say goodbye to her. My Mother will not let me get her and give her to a farm.

What would you do if you were my Mother?

Love,
Joan S———

Dear President,

I have got a picture of you. How is your family. I think the baby is cute. How old is he now? It seems like such a long time. How is your family? I am eight years old. I will be in the third grade. We have got two dogs, two cats and may get another one and we are going to get a hamster for sure. My girl friend is going to give me a hamster.

Thank you.

Sincerely
Lee S———

Dear Mr. Kennedy,

I have heard some of your speeches and I liked them. How are you and your family. I'm ok. Do you have any pets. I have one stupid cat that is afraid of the vacuum cleaner.
Say hello to Caroline and your wife for me.

Love
Mickey G———

Dear President Kennedy,

How are you?
I am fine.
I have rote to you before.
I have a black puppy
His name is Happy
He is a bull dog
He is 10 month old
Please send me a letter and a picture.

George G———

Dear Mr. President,

I read an article about all the animals you receive as gifts and have to give away. I would like very much to provide a home for any of the following: a kitten, mice, rabbits, pidgeons, hamsters, Guineau pigs, birds, monkeys, etc. If, when you find that you can't keep an animal, please remember me.

My ambition is to be a vetrinarian. I have white mice, which I give to a nearby research clinic as they could multiply.

Could you suggest someone I could write to for help? Maybe I could do something for your Agricultural dept. or something, in some small way.

Mary M———

Dear President Kennedy,

My name is Cindy C———. I like horses very very much and I wanted to know if Carolin has a shetland pony? I live in San Francisco California and I like it here very much.

My age is 10 on May 14th. I was promised a horse when I was eleven, how about that.

What is Caroline's favorite pet?

Yours truly
Cindy C———

Dear President Kennedy,

I would like to have your oppinion on the subject of animals. Do they have any brains.

Dorothy E———

P.S. Please answer

Thank you

Dear President,

When my dog, Pal, has her puppys do you want any for the army. I read in the paper where they use them in the Canine Corp. I could send you one.

Peter A———

Dear Mr. President,

I know that the White House is a good place. I wish I could be president too. I have a dog named Happy. Do you have a dog?

Sincerely
Robert S———

Dear Mr. President,

I would very much like to know if the United States of America will be using homing pidgeons in case of an atomic war as they were used in World Wars i and ii. From what I know these wonderful birds played an important part in saving thousands of lives during the first war by carrying a message for help even though it had been wounded.

Yours truly,
Jonathan P———

Dear President Kennedy,

Is the United States ever going to send a man to space. I am 12 years old and would like to go if their was enough air and fuel to get me safely back to earth.

How do you like the house you live in know? I wish I could speak to you in person.

Do you like snakes? I have a 4 foot snake.

Your truly
Jewel R———

Dear President Kennedy,

I live on a farm. With cows, calfes, dogs, a horse and rabbitts. I have a nice home, it is a new house. I have one sister her name is Claudia. Mommy is Molly. Daddy is Jack. I am in the fifth grade.

I am ten years old going on 11 on January 20th. We have a girl calf named Jackie named after you and your wife.

How is Caralyn? I hope she is fine. I suppose you have lots of work to do in the White House. Do you have a T.V. Sorry I have to go.

Love,
Linda H———

. . . named after you and your wife.

Dear Mr. Kennedy,

My brother said you love horses like me. I thought you might hang this horse picture in your room.

Yours sincerely
Paul G———

Dear Mr. Kennedy

I know your very busy with other letters and your everyday work but I'd like to know if I may have a picture of Carolines dogs.

Love,
Eric H———

Dear President Kennedy

How would you like to have a baby kitten. They will be able to leave their mother on the 10th of October.

Sincerely
Eddie T———

Dear Mr. President,

I want to thank you for the very nice letter that was sent to me. A lot of things have happened to us since your last letter. Our mother cat had five kittens. Two of them have stripes so mom named one of them J.B. short for jailbird.

My brother just had a birthday and he is eight years old. Once again I want to thank you for your letter.

Your friend
Tod S———

8

The Autograph Hunters

Collecting autographs is still as popular a childhood hobby as it was fifty years ago and for youngsters today, President Kennedy's autograph appears to rank in the same league with Mickey Mantle's, Fabian's or Captain Kangaroo's autograph.

Requesting the President's autograph—on a piece of paper or a picture—may be a routine affair for most people, but not for the children in these letters to the President. They approach collecting President Kennedy's autograph with a determination only children can bring to such a challenge.

The youngsters ask for autographs and pictures not only of President Kennedy but of Caroline and Mrs. Kennedy.

But the President's autograph has to be the real McCoy—no mass produced facsimiles for these children.

The simple request for the autograph of the President of the United States becomes as complex and involved a situation as the first day of school for many of the young correspondents in these letters.

Dear President Kennedy

Please send me a bigness sise picheur of you with coloor in it.

Thank you
Billy C———

Dear Mr. President,

Would you please send me your audigraph. I need it for a scavanger hunt.

Yours truly,
Fred C———

Dear President,

I would like you to send me some pictures or snapshots of different parts of the White House. They would come in handy in my school work. Thank you.

Yours truly,
Lynda D———

Dear Mr. President,

I would be very happy if you would send me a picture of each of the members of your family and a picture of the congress. And may I have a copy of the picture of you that was printed in the July issue of Seventeen? located on page 100. If you cannot send the pictures may I have a letter on White House stationary.

Sincerely
Natalie D———

Dear Mr. President,

I always try to watch all of your speeches. I think your very handsome. Your wife is very beautiful and your children are the cutest things. Would you please send me a dollar and a picture of you and your family with your autograph and wifes autograph.

Please send me some of your wifes beauty secrets.

Barbara S———

Dear President John F. Kennedy
President of the United States

Thank you very much for the picture you gave me.
We are to find a frame for it. So until I do find a
frame we are keeping it out of reach of everybody.

Yours truly
Susan F———

Dear Mr. President,

I would like a picture of the whole family and yor favorite dish.

Sincerely yours
Joan C———

Dear President Kennedy,

I am just writing a few lines to say hello. May I please have a picher of you and would you please sende your name in front of the picher.

Your friend
Jack C———

Dear Mr. Kennedy,

My name is Nancy C———. I am ten years old and I will be going to the fifth grade. I would like a picture of you an a map of Washington an anything else you could give me.

Your friend,
Nancy C———

Dear President Kennedy,

Thank you for your picture. I am the only one who has one on my block. All the kids look at it. They are jealous.

Thank you
Peggy H———

Dear Mr. President,

It is an honor to live in a country where I can write to the President. All I ask is that I get some reply before the 29th of September. If it is at all possible could you please honor my request and sign in your personal writing your signature.

Thank you
Martin G———

Dear Pres Kennedy

I think Caroline is such a cute little girl and your wife is so attractive and so are you President Kennedy. John (the baby) is adorable.

If you do send the pictures I would like to know Carolines and little Johns birthday so I could send them a card.

Your friend,
Laurie G———

Dear Mr. Kennedy,

I passed your house on Thursday. I wish you were taking your walk maybe I would have seen you.

Please send me a picture of you so I can remember you until I die.

Love
Bobby P————

Dear Sirs,

Could you send me the Presidents and Vice-Presidents calling cards signed on the back.

Yours truly,
Jerry S————

Dear Mr. Kennedy,

I am sending a page from my autograph book. I would like your autograph. Please send the page back when you are finished.

Marie P————

Dear Sirs,

Please, if possible, send me a photograph of Caroline Kennedy that has been sent from the White House to others upon request. This would be sincerely appreciated because I adore Miss Kennedy.
Thank you so much.

So Sincerely,
Melissa C———

Dear Sir,

A lot of my friends have written to Nixon and received pictures. If possible I'd like a picture of your family and yourself. My parents think you are doing a fine job and so do most Nixon fans.

Sincerely yours,
Mary F———

Dear President,

I would like to have your wife's and your autograph, if I may. Also I would like to have some
scribbles from Caroline and all the information I
could have on your family. If you have any animals
may I have a picture of them.

Sincerely
Carol L————

Dear Mr. Kennedy,

I have a friend would like a picture of you and
Mrs. Kennedy and Caroline sitting together. My
girl friend and I would like a separate picture of
you and Mrs. Kennedy. I think Caroline is the
cutest thing in the world.

A good American,
Dean

Dear President Kennedy,

I would like very much to have a photograph of you and your family and an ORIGINAL autograph.

Sincerely yours,
Andrew H———

Dear Mr. President,

Will you please send me a picture of you and your pretty wife.

I have a book with pictures of all the presidents starting with President Washington but I don't have one of you. And I would like to have one of you and Mrs. Kennedy to put on the front of my book as a cover.

Your pal,
Robert G———

Dear Mr. President,

My friend and I would very much to have your autograph, the vice-presidents autograph, and the autograph of some important friends of yours.

We would like to have a letter saying that you gave them to us and that they are not fakes. We would also like to have two congressional records for July 15, 1961.

If you would send these we would be very grateful. Thank you.

Sincerely
Patty M———

Dear Mr. Kennedy,

How are you? Do you still have the letter Lou E——— sent you? Well Lou is my cousin. Please send me a picture like you sent him.

Bill S———

Mr. Kennedy,

Dear Mr. President,

I would like for you to be my pen pal please. I am 9 years old. My mother and daddy voted for you to be president.

Write to me every month if you are going to be my pen pal. I will write to you back every month.

Love,
John H———

P.S. I am sending you a picture of me. Please send me a picture of you.

Dear Mr. President

Please send me spearate pictures of you, Jackie, Caroline and one of Jack Jr. if you have one. I would like the pictures to be wallett size.

A citizen and a friend,
Marie T———

Dear Mr. President,

I am in the fourth grade. I think you are a good President. I voted for you and my Mom voted for you but Dad voted for Nixon.

We were praying for you that you would be a good President and we were praying for peace.

I would appreciate if you would send me your autograph and we are putting a bomb shelter in our bacente.

Sincerely yours
John P———

Dear Mr. Kennedy,

Would you please send me your autograph and picture. I am 10 years old and am passing into the fifth grade. I am sick.

Yours truly
Lois S————

I am sick.

9

Young Citizens Look at the World Situation

Perhaps the most revealing thing we uncovered about our children in selecting the letters for this book is that no matter how young they are, the threat of war hangs heavy over their hearts.

Literally hundreds of letters pour into the White House every week from youngsters expressing their concern about the present international situation.

Children from all over the country—seven, eight, nine years of age—are worried. Not just about getting a few extra pennies for their allowance or a new wheel for the bicycle—but about the world today and where it is heading.

In a sense it is tragic that minds so young should have to concern themselves with problems so grave.

Still, because they are children—with a unique approach to everything—they have their own thoughts on how to change the Cold War and on how the President should handle the Russians.

Many of the letters touch on the world situation with unusual suggestions that the young writers are convinced the President should incorporate in our foreign policy immediately.

If they had their way many of them would lower the army enlistment age to nine—because they want to help.

From the tone of the letters the President has re-received from our young people it is obvious that patriotism starts at a very early age.

All of the letters obviously come from the heart—the heart of our very youngest citizenry who seem to have decided that their wiser adult leaders need some help.

Dear Mr. President

I would like to write you a letter to thank you about the way you are taking care of everything about this war bussiness.

Thomas G———

Dear President Kennedy

I am 8 years old.
I want to ask you a question.
Why do we have to have a war?
Please answer my question.

Yours truly
Kenneth S———

Dear Mr. President,

I am only nine years old and so I found your speech hard to understand. I think one day in the near future you should dedicate a speech (about what is going on in the world) to children and make it easy for us to understand.

Sincerely yours,
Laura D———

Dear President Kennedy,

How come you don't let kids go fite the Rusins? I am olney 9 years old.

Love
John C———

Dear Sir,

I would like to know how a person under age for the army can help the United States in the on-coming months. I think you need my help.

A good citizen
Fred G———

Dear President Kennedy

I am nine years old but I know more than most other nine year olds. I know what war, killing and suffering are. I understand your problems.

Your pal,
Stephen L———

Dear President Kennedy,

I wish we didn't have any war. I have some ideas of my own. I wish you could sit down and talk about it with Russia.
Do you have any thoughts about it?

Sincerely yours,
Bert D———

Dear John F. Kennedy,

I want to stop all wars but I can't because I'm too little. I'm 7½ years old. I don't like wars. I think its stupid and nobody can make me change my mind. And if you can I want you to write to me a letter and tell me what you think of wars.

Your friend
David R———

Dear Mr. President,

My name is Nancy P———. Today when I was watching television I heard that Russia launched another man into space.

Later in the day I got to thinking why the United States can't send a man in an orbit, if Russia can do it why can't we. All it takes is hard work and ambition.

Mr. President what will happen if Russia gets to the moon first? Will they say they own it or will they share it with us?

How can we build bomb shelters in New Orleans.

Sincerely yours,
Nancy P———

Dear President Kennedy

My name is Kevin. I am 10 years old and I enjoy all sports mainly swimming.

What I wanted to say was I love by mother and my family and so do most people and I was wondering if you could try extra hard to stop the trouble that's brewing.

Yours truly
Kevin P———

P.S. I think you make a swell president

Dear President Kennedy,

My name is Scott H———, I live in Dallas, Texas. I wrote to discuss a problem with you.

My problem is about these little wars between little nations. I think myself that we should not help them unless they write down in paper that they would help us when or if we have a war against Russia or some other nation. Please write back, if you have time, and tell me your oppinion on my problem.

Yours truly
Scott H———

Dear Mr. Kennedy,

I am 10 years old. And was born after World War 11. And many, many more children were too. These children never live through a war. I know I haven't had to. I also scare easy. Also your address to the nation scared me. Please don't have a war.

An American,
Lloyd J———

I scare easy.

Dear Sirs,

I know this letter will probably never reach the Presidents desk but I am sure he has assistants as capable of answering my questions as he is.

I would like to know if the poor people have enough food to eat in case of war.

I am only 9 years old but I am aware that war is near.

Shirley R———

Dear Mr. President,

My name is Marion N———. I am writing this letter too you with my girl friend Betsy. I know we are just kids and especially now in 61. You probably will read this and forget about it but whoever is reading it please try to understand this letter. We watch the news and try to understand the reason why we would have a 3rd world war. In your own words please try to answer this question? Also why would anybody want a war? Who do you think would start it? If the Russians start the war will they pick on us first?

Who has strongest weapons between us and Russia?

Please excuse the handwriting
from two loyal fans
Love
Marion N——— and
Betsy P———

Dear Mr. President,

I am eleven years old and every night I worry. I worry about what will happen tomorrow, not so much as tomorrow, but as the future.

What will be left of this wonderful world in ten years if someone presses the button? What will be left of you and your family? All I'm asking for is *please think* before you press the button, please.

Sincerely yours
Roger N———

Dear John F. Kennedy,

I am 9 years of age and I think you are a nice man. So please listen to what I have to say.

God gave us the earth to live on and he gave us the moon to give us light at night. If he would have wanted us to live on the moon he would have put us there. So if you want to reach the moon you have to pray to God and ask him for help.

Why do we have war? We should not try to make changes on the earth. God does the changing not man. If God wants changes made he'll make them but we can't.

I would like for you to write me back. I think that this will help our world.

With love
Anne S———

Dear Mr. President,

With the world situation what it is I believe that
if a campain was started with the theme of George
M. Cohans patriotic songs men of the United States
would relize their duty to their country.

Sincerely yours
Gloria C———

Dear President Kennedy,

My name is Holly M—— (I'm a girl) and I'm 10 years old.

I am quite confused about the situation between Russia and the United States and I thought maybe you could help me a bit.

I have asked many people about this tough situation, though getting diffrent replies. I was thinking, which one of them was right and that was the time I thought of writing to you.

Yours truly,
Holly

Dear Mr. President,

Before a baseball game the National Anthem is played, which brings a thought to my mind.

What if another flag of another country would fly over the United States instead of our own wonderful Stars and Stripes.

This is why I am writing so this thought would never come true.

Please write soon if it is possible so that I may know what I can do to continue in making the United States a world power for a democratic way of life.

Bradford R——

Dear President Kennedy,

My name is Alfred M————. I am 10 and live in New York City.

I am writing to ask you about a very important matter. Krushev wants the whole world. The only way he can have it is if we have a war. That would cause world destruction.

I think that both of you should think twice.

Please tell me if I am right.

Yours truly
Alfred M————

Dear President Kennedy,

I am 11 years old and I'm writing because I want to tell you something about this cold war thats getting pretty hot.

I know this has never been done before but could you ask former President Eisenhower and former President Truman to have a conference with you and let them give their ideas and suggestions to help end this cold war.

I am sure a lot of people feel the same way I do.

Thank you for reading
my letter
Grace F————

Mr. Kennedy,

I am 9 years old. I don't like the plans you are planning. I am too young to die.

Signed
Robert S———

The White House Mail

The White House mailroom is certainly one of the busiest places in the nation's capitol. At least, that was the distinct impression I received while spending many hours there selecting the letters for this book.

Consider the fact that on the average more than 20,000 letters and postcards arrive at the White House mailroom every week—all addressed to the President of the United States. This number of letters places John F. Kennedy in the number one spot among Presidents in terms of the amount of mail received weekly. Of these 20,000 letters more than 2,000 are from children.

In order to take care of this tremendous amount of mail the Post Office Department makes four daily deliveries to the White House. The mailroom is located in a series of connecting rooms in the basement of the Executive Office building just across the driveway which leads to the West Wing of the White House.

Shortly after arrival the mail is opened and the letters from children are then deposited in a special room used only for mail to the President from his young correspondents. Here the letters are sorted by state and subject matter by the extremely competent White House mailroom staff.

From the "children's room" most of the letters are quickly forwarded to the White House correspondence section. There a team of highly skilled letter-writers answer them on behalf of the President and in accordance with his instructions.

Very unusual letters are sent to the President's immediate staff so that Mr. Kennedy may look at them himself if his crowded schedule permits.

This policy led to the now celebrated story which concerned a particular letter that arrived in the White House mailroom one day. It was in a child's handwriting, and it read:

> Dear Jack,
>> I would like to see you soon.
>> By Jack.
>
>> Bobby

Ordinarily this type of letter would not be called to the President's personal attention. However, an alert member of the White House mail staff noticed that the return address on this letter was McLean, Virginia. Since the Robert Kennedys lived in McLean, she had a hunch that perhaps this might be a letter to the President from Bobby Kennedy Jr., the seven-year-old-son of the Attorney General, who is, of course, the President's brother.

Her hunch proved to be correct. A few days later Bobby Kennedy Jr. was ushered into the President's office where he presented his Uncle Jack with a gift—a pet salamander.

Not all youngsters who write to the President can expect such action but the chances that the President will read their letters are getting better. President Kennedy recently gave instructions that each day every fiftieth letter that is received at the White House mailroom is to be sent directly to his personal staff. In this way the President can keep in closer contact with what Americans have to say concerning key issues.

Judging by the letters from youngsters selected for this book the President has a very good idea about what our youngest citizens are thinking and saying these days.

As a matter of fact, I trust that after reading these letters—we all do.